HAL•LEONARD®

DRUM
PLAY-ALONG

AUDIO
ACCESS
INCLUDED

'80s ROCK

VOL. 8

T0081511

Tracking, mixing, and mastering by Jake Johnson
& Bill Maynard at Paradyme Productions
Drums by Scott Schroedl
Guitars by Doug Boduch
Bass by Tom McGirr
Keyboards by Warren Wiegratz

PLAYBACK+
Speed • Pitch • Balance • Loop

To access audio visit:
www.halleonard.com/mylibrary

Enter Code
7787-6822-9753-7881

ISBN 978-1-4234-1596-1

HAL•LEONARD®

For all works contained herein:
Unauthorized copying, arranging, adapting, recording, Internet posting, public performance,
or other distribution of the music in this publication is an infringement of copyright.
Infringers are liable under the law.

Visit Hal Leonard Online at
www.halleonard.com

Contact Us:
Hal Leonard
7777 West Bluemound Road
Milwaukee, WI 53213
Email: info@halleonard.com

In Europe contact:
Hal Leonard Europe Limited
42 Wigmore Street
Marylebone, London, W1U 2RN
Email: info@halleonardeurope.com

In Australia contact:
Hal Leonard Australia Pty. Ltd.
4 Lentara Court
Cheltenham, Victoria, 3192 Australia
Email: info@halleonard.com.au

CONTENTS

Cult of Personality

Words and Music by William Calhoun,
Corey Glover, Muzz Skillings and Vernon Reid

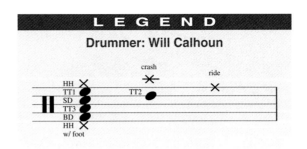

Intro
Moderate Rock ♩ = 92

(Guitar)

1. Look in my

Verse

eyes, _____ what do you see? ____   The cult of per-son-al — i - ty.

I know your an - ger,   I know your dreams. __   I've

been ev-'ry-thing you wan - na be. _____   Oh, __   I'm the   cult of per-son-al — i - ty.

Guitar Solo

Verse

6

Bridge

Ne - on — lights, No - bel — Prize. — When a lead - er — speaks, — that

lead - er — dies. _____ He won't — have — to fol - low — me, —

on - ly — you — can set you free. _____

Guitar Solo

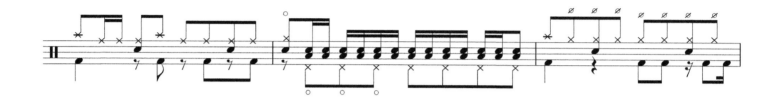

3. You gave me for -

Verse

- tune, you gave me fame. _ You gave me pow - er in your _ God's

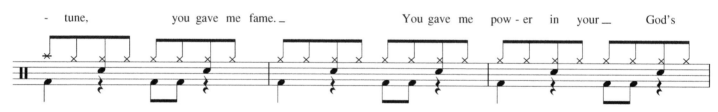

name. I'm ev -'ry per - son _ you need to be. _ Oh. _

Chorus

I'm _ the _ cult _ of _ per - son -

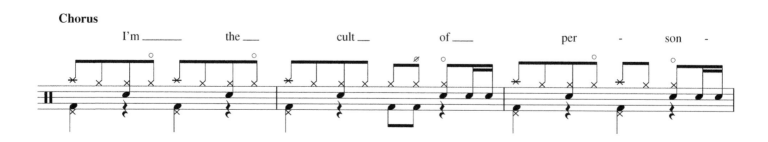

- al - i - ty. I am the cult of, I am the cult of,

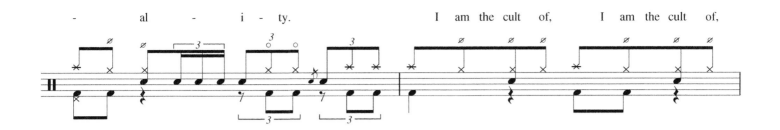

I am the cult of, I am the cult of, I am the cult of, I am the cult of,

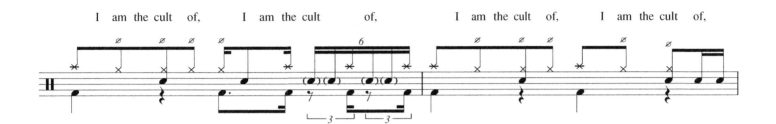

I am the cult of, I am the cult of per - son - al - i - ty. _____ "Ask

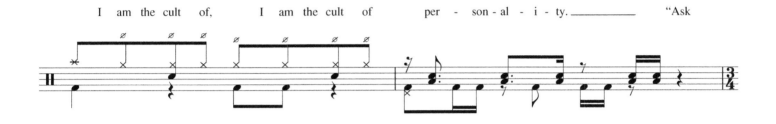

Outro
Double-time feel

not what your coun - try can do for you..."

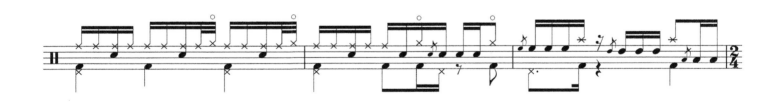

"The only thing we have to fear is, fear itself."

Heaven's on Fire

Words and Music by Paul Stanley and Desmond Child

Intro
Moderate Rock ♩ = 126

Verse

1. I look at you and my blood boils hot.

I feel my tem-per'-ture rise. ___ I want it all; give me

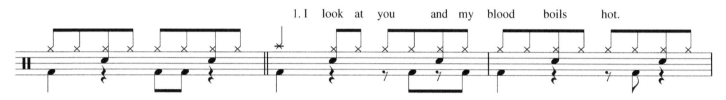

what you've got. ___ There's hun-ger in your eyes. ___

Pre-Chorus

I'm get-ting clos-er, ba-by; hear me breathe. _

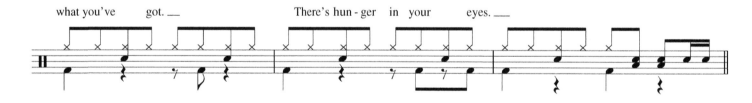

You know the way to give me what I need. _

start to   tease. ___   You can bring the dev - il   to his   knees. _   Feel _

Chorus

___ my heat   tak - ing you high-er.   Burn ___ with me.   Heav - en's on   fire.   Paint _

___ the sky   with ___ de - sire.   An - gel   fly.   Heav - en's on   fire.   Whoa. _

Bridge

Heav - en's on   fire. ___

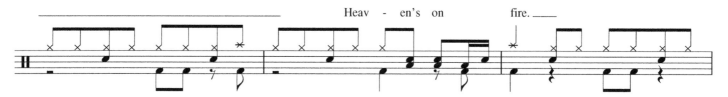

Whoa. _____   Heav - en's on   fire. ___

Whoa. _____

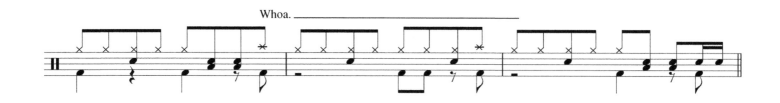

Interlude

Pre-Chorus

I'm get-ting clos-er, ba-by; hear me breathe. _

You know the way to give me what I need. _

D.S. al Coda

Coda

Just let me love you; I could nev-er leave. _ Feel _ - en's on fire. Feel _

Outro-Chorus

2nd & 3rd times, substitute Fill 1

___ my heat tak-ing you high-er. Burn ___ with me. Heav-en's on fire. Paint _

Repeat and fade

___ the sky with ___ de-sire. An-gel fly. Heav-en's on fire. Feel _

Fill 1

Rock of Ages

Words and Music by Joe Elliott, Richard Savage,
Richard Allen, Steve Clark, Peter Willis and Robert Lange

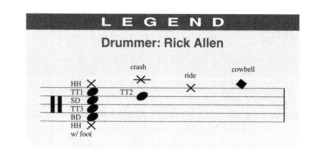

Intro
Moderately ♩ = 105

Gun - ter, glieb - en, glauch - en, glob - en.

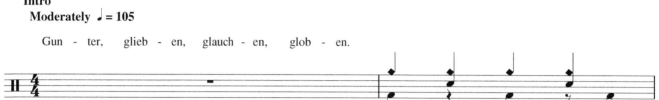

Al - right.   I got some-thing to say,

yeah. __   It's bet-ter to burn   out,   yeah,

than fade _ a - way. _____   Al - right. __

Ow.

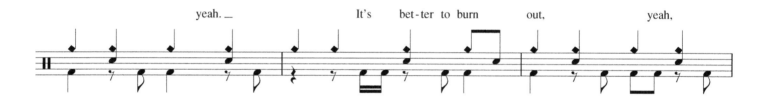

Gon-na start a fire. _   C'-mon.

Verse

1. Rise up, gath - er 'round. _ Rock this place to the ground. _

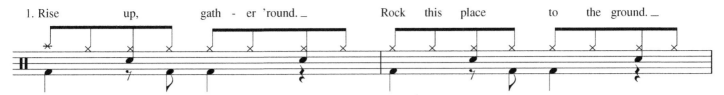

Burn it up, __ let's go for broke. _ Watch the night __ go up in __ smoke. _

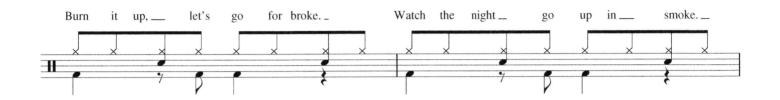

Rock on. _____ Rock on! _____ Drive me cra - zi - er, _____ no __

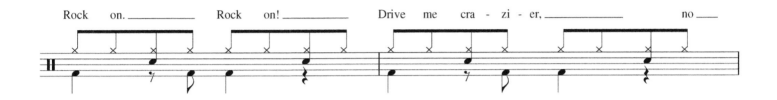

ser - e - nade, _ no fire bri - gade, _ just a py - ro - ma - ni - a, ___ c' - mon.

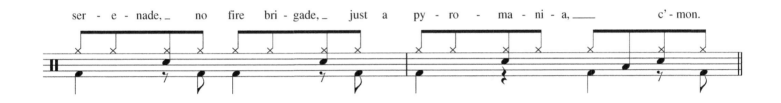

Bridge

What do you want? _ What do you want? _ I __ want __ rock 'n' roll. _

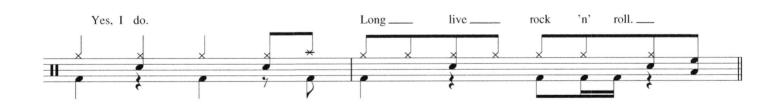

Yes, I do. Long ___ live ___ rock 'n' roll. ___

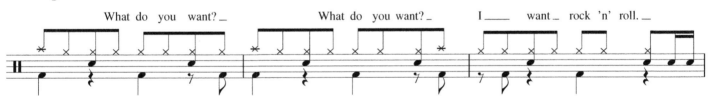

Verse

2. Oh, let's go, let's strike a light. _ We're gon - na blow _ like dy - na - mite. _

I don't care ____ if it takes all ____ night, _ gon - na set this ___ town a - light, ___ c'-mon.

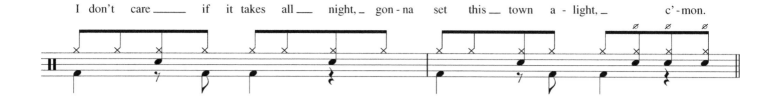

Bridge

What do you want? _   What do you want? _   I ____ want _ rock 'n' roll. _

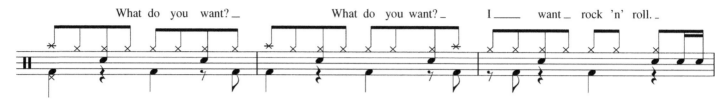

Al - right!   Long _ live _ rock 'n' roll. _   Oh, _____ yeah, _ yeah!

𝄋 Chorus

2nd time, substitute Fill 1

Rock of a - ges,   rock of a - ges,   still ___ roll - in',

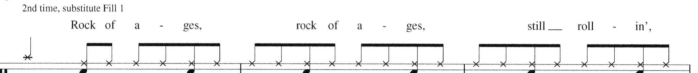

keep a roll - in'.   Rock of a - ges,   rock of a - ges,

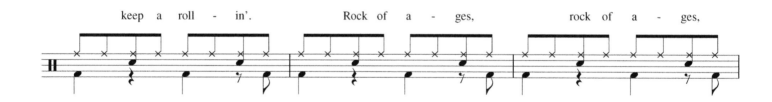

still ___ roll - in',   rock 'n' roll - in'.   We got the pow - er,

Fill 1

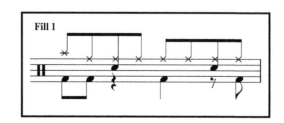

we got __ the glo - ry.   Just say you need it,   and __ if you need it, say

yeah, _____   oo, yeah. ___   Ha, ha, ha, ha, ha, ha.   Now

Verse

lis - ten to me.   3. I'm burn - in', burn - in',   I ___ got the fe - ver. __

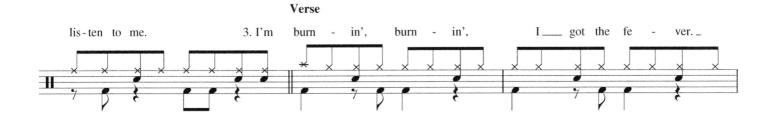

I know for sure   there ain't __ no __ cure.   So feel __ it, don't fight   it,

go __ with the flow. __   Gim-me, gim-me, gim-me, gim-me, gim-me one more __ for the road, __   yeah.

Bridge

What do you want? _____   What do you want? _____

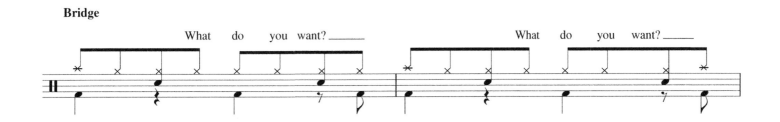

I ___ want __ rock 'n' roll. __   You bet ya!   Long __ live __ rock 'n' roll. __ Ah,

Guitar Solo

yes!

D.S. al Coda

Coda

Outro

yeah. _____   Say __   yeah! _

We're gon - na burn that damn place down, _   whoo, _____

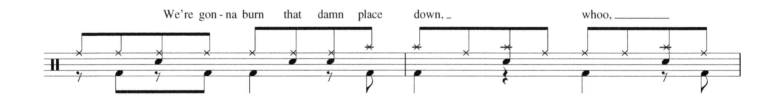

down _ to the ground.

Smokin' in the Boys Room

Words and Music by Michael Koda and Michael Lutz

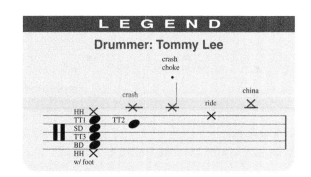

Intro
Moderately ♩ = 140

Spoken: Whew! D'ya ever seem to have one of those days when everyone's on your case, from your teacher all the way

down to your best girlfriend? Well, you know I used to have 'em just about all the time. But I found

a way to get out of it. Let me tell you about... 1. I'm

Verse

sit-tin' in the class - room, think-in' it's a drag. Lis-ten-in' to the teach-er rap
2. Check-in' out the hall, mak-in' sure the coast is clear. Look-in' in the stalls, nah, there

just ain't my bag. ___ But when two bells ___ ring, ___ you know it's my cue. ___ I'm
ain't no-bod-y here. My bud-dies Sixx, Mick and Tom, ___ to

Guitar Solo

3. Well,

Verse

put me to work — in   the school book store   check-out count - er, and I —

Smok-in' in the boy's room. _____ Hey, teach-

- er, don't ya fill me up with your rule, _ 'cause ev-'ry-bod-y knows that

smok-in' ain't al-lowed in school. One more.

Outro-Chorus

Smok-in' in the boy's room. Smok-in' in the boy's room.

Now teach-er, I ain't fool-in' a-round with your rule, _ 'cause

ev-'ry-bod-y knows that smok-in' ain't al-lowed _ in school.

Slower ♩ = 106

rit.

Free time

Shake Me

Words and Music by Tom Keifer

LEGEND

Drummer: Jody Cortez

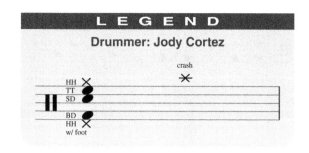

Intro
Moderate Rock ♩ = 135

All   right, ___   yeah.

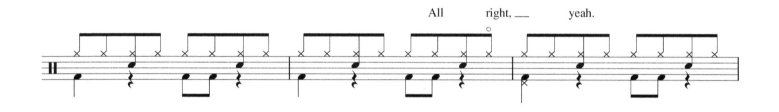

Verse

1. I   met this girl a - round_ quar - ter to ten. _____   We made it once she said,

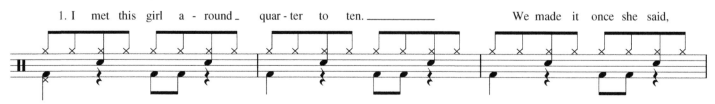

All night long, ___ ba - by.

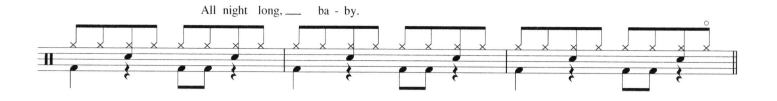

Verse

2. Screamed and scratched and rolled ___ out of the bed, ___ I nev - er real - ly got her

out of my head. ___ And now and then she makes those ___ so - cial calls, ___

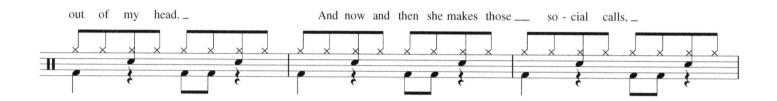

gives me a squeeze, gets me kick - in' the walls. ___ Now let me tell ya, it

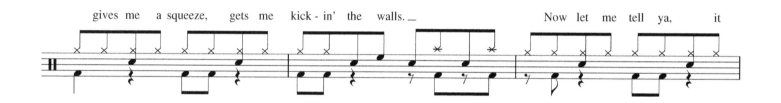

still feels tight, _____ and we were shak - in' af - ter ev - er - y bite. ___

I feel her com - in' in the mid - dle of the night. ___ Scream - in' high - er.

Chorus

"Shake me all _____ night." She said,

Interlude

Shake me.

Shake me.

Shake me.

Shake me.

Talk Dirty to Me

Words and Music by Bobby Dall, Brett Michaels,
Bruce Johannesson and Rikki Rockett

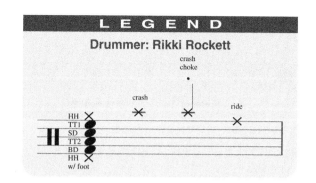

Intro
Moderate Rock ♩ = 160

Verse

3. You know I call you, I call ___ you on the tel - e - phone, ___

___ I'm on - ly hop - in' that you're home ___

so I can hear ___ you when you

say those words to me ___ and

whis - per so ___ soft - ly. ___ I've got - ta hear ___

___ you. 'Cause, ba - by, we'll ___ be

Chorus

at the drive - in, ___ in the old ___

man's Ford, _ be - hind the bush - es, _

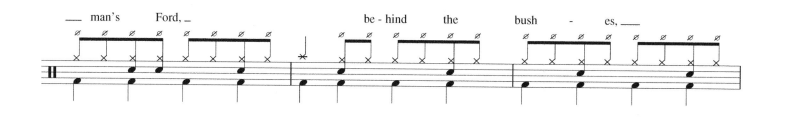

uh, till I'm scream-in' for more. _ Down _ the

base - ment, _ lock the cel - lar door, _ and

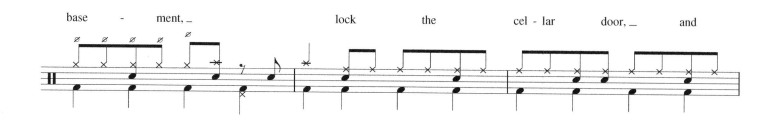

ba - by, _ talk dirt - y to me. _

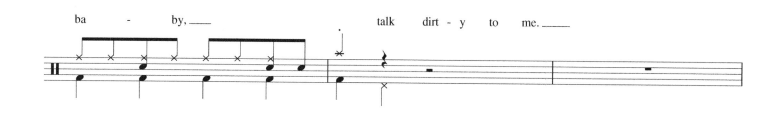

C. C., pick up that gui - tar and, uh, talk to me, yeah!

Guitar Solo

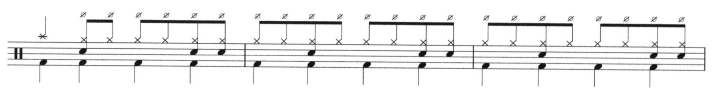

You Give Love a Bad Name

Words and Music by Jon Bon Jovi, Richie Sambora and Desmond Child

Intro
Moderate Rock ♩ = 123

Shot through the heart, _ and you're to _ blame, dar - lin', you give _ love _____ a

bad _ name.

Verse
1. An an - gel's smile _ is what you sell. You

prom - ised me heav - en, then put me through hell. _ Chains of _ love _ got a hold   on   me.   When pas - sion's a pris - on you can't break   free.

Pre-Chorus

Whoa, _____ you're a load - ed gun. __   Yeah. __

Whoa, _____ there's no - where to run.

No one can save me, the dam - age is done.

𝄋 **Chorus**

Shot through the heart, _ and you're to ____ blame. You give love _____ a

bad name, bad name. I play my part, ___ and you play your ___ game.

To Coda ⊕

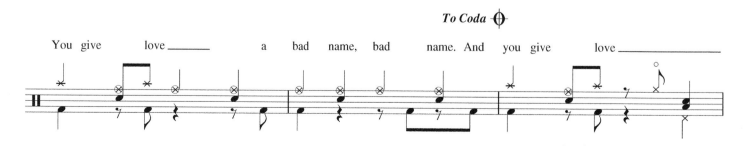

You give love _____ a bad name, bad name. And you give love _____

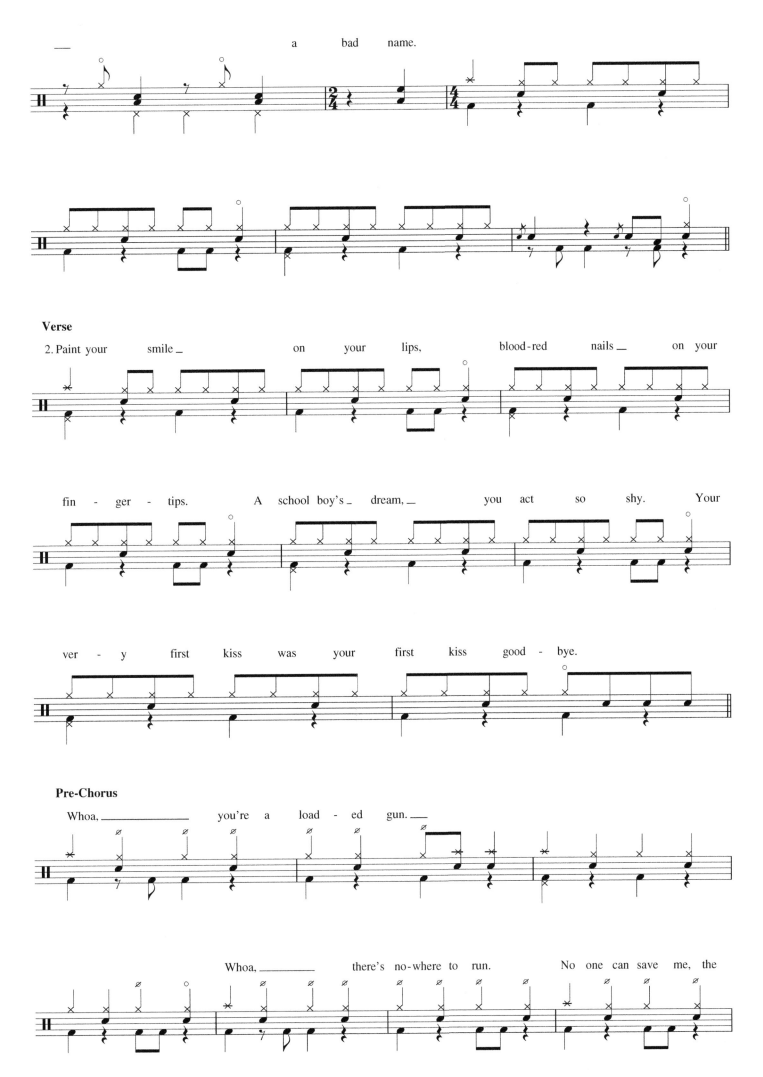

a bad name.

Verse

2. Paint your smile __ on your lips, blood-red nails __ on your

fin - ger - tips. A school boy's __ dream, __ you act so shy. Your

ver - y first kiss was your first kiss good - bye.

Pre-Chorus

Whoa, _____ you're a load - ed gun. __

Whoa, _____ there's no-where to run. No one can save me, the

We're Not Gonna Take It

Words and Music by Daniel Dee Snider

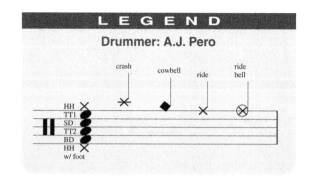

§ **Verse**

2nd time, substitute Fill 1

1. We've got the right to choose _ and there ain't no
2. *See additional lyrics*

way we'll lose _ it. _ This is our life; __ this is __ our song. _

2nd time, substitute Fill 2

__ We'll fight the

pow'rs that be _ just. Don't pick our des - ti - ny, _ 'cause _

To Coda ⊕

you don't know us, ___ you don't _ be - long. _

Chorus

We're not gon - na take _ it,

No, we ain't gon - na take ____ it.   We're not gon - na take _

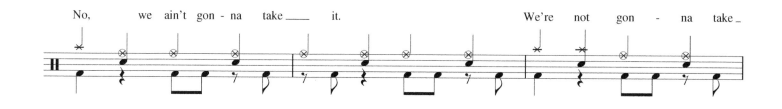

D.S. al Coda

____ it   an - y - more. _____

Coda

____   your best   won't ____ do.

Bridge

(Whoa, _____   whoa.) _____

_____ We're   right, (Yeah.) _ we're   free, (Yeah.) _ we'll

fight.   (Yeah.) _ You'll   see. _____   Whoa. _____

Chorus

We're not gon - na take ____ it.   No,   we ain't gon - na take _

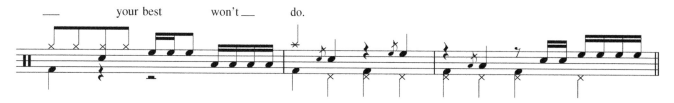

44

Guitar Solo

Bridge

(Whoa, _____   whoa.) _____

_____   We're   right,   (Yeah.) _ we're   free,   (Yeah.) _ we'll

fight.   (Yeah.) _ You'll   see. _____

Breakdown-Chorus

We're not gon - na take __ it.   No,   we ain't gon - na take __ it.

We're not gon - na take __ it   an - y - more. ____

Chorus

We're not gon - na take __ it.   No,   we ain't gon - na take __ it.

Additional Lyrics

2. Oh, you're so condescending.
   Your gall is never-ending.
   We don't want nothin'; not a thing from you.
   Your life is trite and jaded,
   Boring and confiscated.
   If that's your best, your best won't do.